the ballad of
bill spinks' bedstead
& other poems

Pam Ayres

the ballad of
bill spinks' bedstead
& other poems

Illustrations by Don Roberts

SEVERN
HOUSE

First U.K. Publication 1981
by Severn House Publishers Ltd
144-146 New Bond Street, London W1Y 9FD

Design and Photography Rob Burt

British Library Cataloguing in Publication Data
Ayres, Pam
  The Ballad of Bill Spinks' Bedstead
  1. Title
  821'.914   PR6051.Y64

ISBN 07278 2018 4

Printed in Great Britain by The Anchor Press
and bound by Wm Brendon & Son Ltd
both of Tiptree, Essex.

contents

The Rat Resuscitation Rhyme

I found a dead rat in our woodshed,
I found it at quarter to eight,
I tried to give it the kiss of life
But I'd left it ten minutes too late.

The Swimming Song

I like to swim
I'll meet you after school
It keeps us trim
I'll see you down the pool
It keeps us fit
Watch out we're on the prowl
We do our bit
Talcum powder and a towel
Both great and small
Watch us on the diving board
Life savers all
Duke of Edinburgh's Award
If we're around
We're demons in the drink
You won't get drowned
We never ever sink.

We swim like fish
Cod, kipper, cockle, carp
Here, there, gone, swish!
Oh play it on your harp
And diving too
In the deep dark dregs
Just me and you
We'll be laughing at the legs
Just name the stroke
Oh, the butterfly and crawl
And I'm your bloke
Will you give me back my ball?
I love to spring
Plunge plink plonk paddle
It makes me sing
Tra la diddle daddle.

We're in the shower
Shampoo soap scrub
For half an hour
Rub a dub a dub a dub
Do you know that
Dad gave me fifty pence
You aren't half fat
Ouch! Eek! No offence!
It's great to swim
Never any pain or ache
It keeps us slim
Would you like a piece of cake?
So after school
If you have an hour to spend
Come to the pool
We'll race you to the end.

All Dust and Rubble

I have got the builders in —
It's not a lot of trouble;
Choking in the dust
And falling over in the rubble.
But I shall see much clearer
Once my lintels have been raised,
And come the revolution
We shall all be double glazed.

Oh they're hacking at the plaster
And they're tearing up the floor.
Don't go out! The painter's
Slapping primer on the door.
My little dog gets in the way
They say, "Come out me dear!"
If I'm in the room —
If not, they kick her in the rear.

I'm the only one who doesn't have
A job to do.
Everybody's sprinting past
With chunks of four by two.
I make the tea at ten
And then I make some more at three
And while I'm on the subject
Would *you* like a cup of tea?

Still, the plumber's very nice
Although his hair is white with dust.
Chase me if you like
But chase the pipework if you must.
Every window's open
The wind is like a knife
And the Sparks is cracking
Pornographic jokes about his wife.

They switched off the electric,
They didn't tell my why.
The central heating boiler's
Stiff and cold and so am I.
But I mustn't be downhearted!
I'll wash up and make a drink!
But there isn't any water
And there isn't any sink.

Oh, wrap me in a dustsheet
Till my wood has all been sealed,
Till my tiles have all been grouted
And my stonework all revealed.
Eradicate my infestations!
Fill my cavities with foam!
Normal life will be resumed
When the builders have gone home.

The Ballad of Bill Spinks' Bedstead

Bill Spinks gazed round his bedroom
From the ceiling to the floor,
At the ancient bullfight poster
With *him* as the matador.
And something was amiss
That he could not put into words
But in simple language it was this:
He didn't get the birds.

He supposed his furniture
Would never fill a bird with joy:
The bedside cupboard cobbled up
In 'Woodwork' as a boy;
And flapping at the window
Was a tired bit of chintz,
And round the light switch on the wall
Were dirty fingerprints.

Bill Spinks, propped up with pillows,
Gazed about in deep depression —
The bed was half the trouble
It gave such a bad impression.
You could try no acrobatics here
And if by chance you should
The springs played such a melody
It woke the neighbourhood.

It had no padded headboard —
This was wooden, from his mother.
It was eighteen inches high one side
And two foot on the other.
The rocky flocky mattress
Though its origins were dim
Had crippled seven generations
And was hard at work on him.

So Bill Spinks formed a plan
He went methodically about it:
He wrote himself a shopping list
Got up and went without it.
But if he had remembered it
The first instruction read:
Cash your National Savings stamps
And buy yourself a bed!

He stepped into the shop
He had his breakfast in his hand,
It was a mutton sandwich
Strapped up with a rubber band.
And there he bought a bed
Which was fantastic beyond words:
A bed to revolutionise his life
(and get the birds!)

Oh, but what a bed it was
Upholstered all in damson suede,
And when you touched a button
All the quadrasonics played,
And set into the headboard
Ringed in chromium and cork
A clock told you the time
In Bulawayo and New York.

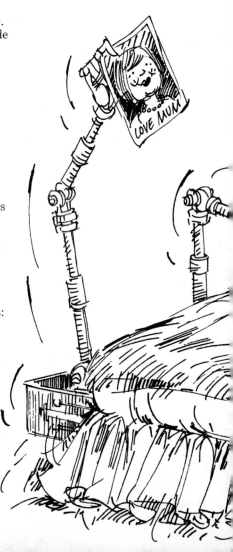

It had an Operations Centre
With a neon-lit console
With a 'phone correctly placed
To get your finger in the hole.
A button for the video,
And if you pressed another
It made a cup of tea
And showed a picture of your mother.

If you pulled a hidden lever
The electric lights all blinked
And a rubber blow-up woman
Stripped off all her clothes and winked.
And in the dead of night
If you should feel the need to go
A claw came out from under
And it offered you the po.

So with the bed installed
Bill Spinks went looking for a mate.
The bed puffed up his ego
Which had flagged so much of late.
He went off down the disco
And the atmosphere was nice
With everybody spitting —
And a few had thrown up twice.

Yes, the Throttlers and the Wrenchers
They were both on stage together,
Punishing their instruments
In glossy wet-look leather.
But it was hard to tell
Because they'd all got so entrenched
Who was doing the throttling
And who was getting wrenched!

But he saw Ms Grippo Millet —
She'd have been the best girl there
If it wasn't for her face, her feet,
Her figure and her hair.
She was the most exquisite creature
Bill Spinks had ever seen:
Half her hair was purple
And the other half was green.

And he danced with Grippo Millet
From the moment that they met
While the Wrenchers' and the Throttlers'
music grew more frenzied yet.
And Bill Spinks said, "Oh Grippo!
Come with me and the spend the night."
And Grippo Millet said, "I'm not like that you know...
All right."

Meanwhile in Bill Spinks' house
The bed was silent and aggrieved.
This was not the kind of setting
For which it had been conceived.
The rain blew in the window
And it pattered on the suede
And the bed thought of the showroom
And it wished it could have stayed.

It could hear Bill Spinks and Grippo
As they carried on below —
The bed sensed what was coming next
And didn't want to know.
But luckily it had
Beneath the damson suede protection
A 90-horsepower engine
With twin carbs and fuel injection.

Now Bill had coaxed his Grippo
To the bottom of the stair
And his hands were turning purple
As he rubbed them through her hair,
And just as Grippo Millet
Was responding to his touch
A sound came from above them
As the bed let in the clutch!

The bed was weary to the mattress
Of the mean and dingy view,
So it slapped itself in gear
And went to look for somewhere new.
It stunned Bill Spinks in passing
With a po jab from the right
And with all the covers flapping
Disappeared into the night.

Grippo watched the apparition
"What the hell was that?" she said,
And Bill Spinks, his head still ringing
Said, "I think it was me bed."
So she stayed to comfort Bill
Because he seemed at such a loss
And the bed has found a lovely home
In a house outside Kings Cross.

The Exiled Gum

Don't water me no more my friend,
Don't water me no more.
I am an exiled Eucalypt
Far from my native shore.
If I'd have been in Sydney
I might have made a show,
But I've been sent to England
And I ain't going to grow.

Don't stand me on the window sill
And pluck out every weed,
Don't sprinkle me with potash
To germinate me seed.
Me little heart is broken
My country was my all
If I can't sprout where the kookaburras shout
Well, I don't want to sprout at all.

I'll never feel the rolling paddy melons
Bump me trunk,
I'll never probe the stubbies there
And get a little drunk.
Not for me the Tasman Sea
To watch the breakers roll
For I am in the window
In a tasteful copper bowl.

And a gum tree's heart's so fearless
He must face the searing drought,
But in this English sitting room
There's not much drought about.
And of the raging bushfires
I do not see a lot
Except for when her husband
Stubs his fag out in me pot!

I need Australian sunshine,
I need the blistering heat,
A wedgetailed eagle on me head
And a wombat at me feet.
I want to grow where Mother stood
I want to be there too.
Oh Mother dear, where are you now?
Gone for a canoe.

Farewell you noble eucalypts
Our roots shall ne'er entwine
Underneath Australia,
For they have potted mine.
Me little shoot has wilted
But it's facing to the east
Good sailing, dearest Mother
From the exiled gum, deceased.

Paul O'Chatberg Grogan

He was Paul O'Chatberg Grogan,
He was manly, he was lean,
The sun had bleached his hair
And it was thick and it was clean.
His eyes were cold as chisels
Far too blue for any man
And when he gazed on women
Well, they clutched their drawers and ran.

He was Paul O'Chatberg Grogan
Of the long athletic stride
With long athletic arms
All down his long athletic side,
With long athletic legs;
And those that knew the family well
Said he had a long athletic
History as well.

He was Paul O'Chatberg Grogan
He could ride and he could hunt
And when he was at Cambridge
He was mustard with a punt.
He could speak in any language
The world had ever known,
And when he got fed up with that
He wrote one of his own.

He was a demon on the squash court
And a tyrant in the gym;
He had a spotted belt in judo
(They'd invented it for him).
And when he hit a cricket ball
The sound was like no other's
For the bat disintegrated
And he had to use his brother's.

Oh, his gaze was always level,
His chin was always square,
His voice was always even
And his teeth were always there.
He drove a Maserati
The fastest he could find
And a little string of broken hearts
All flopped along behind.

A Countess shared his life —
From Spain, with eyes as dark as coals.
They jetted round the world
With him relaxed at the controls.
And she had hair like ebony
And she had skin like gold
With hands that felt like butterflies
And feet that felt the cold.

And she had feather pillows
And she had satin sheets,
And Paul O'Chatberg Grogan
Could perform amazing feats.
The feats he could perform
Cannot be decently revealed
But a chicken house collapsed
A mile behind them in a field.

Here lies Paul O'Chatberg Grogan
Place no headstone, lay no wreath.
One morning in the mirror
He was dazzled by his teeth.
The lonely Maserati
Is silent on the grass
And broken hearts jump up
And dash themselves against the glass.

Arthur Dan Steely, the Novelty Act

Arthur Dan Steely, the Novelty Act,
Stood in the hallway: his cases were packed.
He called to his wife saying, "Leave you I must"
And she clung to the door knob and laughed fit to bust.
He straightened his shoulders and took up his case
Taking a last look around the old place,
He took in the dirt and the cracks and the holes
And said, "When I come back I'll come back in a Rolls."

He opened the door and he walked down the street,
And behind him his wife couldn't stand on her feet.
She laughed and she laughed, she was tickled to death;
And her face ran with tears and she gasped for her breath.
But Arthur Dan Steely, the Novelty Act,
Sat on a bus and his pride was intact,
Mentally checking the props he had taken,
And his faith in his talent was firm and unshaken.

They were holding auditions for Unusual Acts:
Arthur Dan Steely had read all the facts.
He signed at the Stage Door, then boldly beneath
Wrote: Arthur Dan Steely for Tunes on the Teeth!
Yes! It was true! It was his Act alone!
He'd learnt all its foibles as each tooth had grown.
Now, perfectly tuned from the north to the south
They were like a whole orchestra packed in his mouth.

There were singers and dancers and acrobats there
And a director sat in a director's chair
And Arthur Dan Steely he took off his 'mac
And selected a dignified seat, at the back.
The singers did sing and the acrobats leap
And the director peacefully went off to sleep.
And Arthur Dan Steely grew nervous and sat
Patiently waiting and twisting his hat.

At last the address system booming and cracked
Said, "Arthur Dan Steely, the Novelty Act!"
He took up the pencil and switched on the tape
And walked on the stage with his mouth all agape.
He graciously bowed to the people within
And, to show them his instruments, flashed them a grin.
And tuned up a bit in the way of great bands
And everyone covered their mouths with their hands.

Then the music began! It was just like a spur!
He shot round the stage and his feet were a blur,
He tapped them above and he tapped them beneath
And flakes of enamel, they flew off his teeth.
The music was frenzied, he gave it his all!
He gave them Scott Joplin and "After the Ball".
The Director woke up and looked, it was odd
For he covered his eyes up and said, "Oh, Good God!"

He had just reached the point where, to give them a laugh,
He bit that particular pencil in half
When he stopped in his tracks. He was shocked and perplexed·
Oh, surely he hadn't heard someone shout "Next!"
Yes he had! An assistant just waved him away,
As he'd wave at a fly on a hot summer's day.
And onto the stage came a juggling troupe,
The Dinner Plate Whirlers from Old Guadaloupe.

Arthur Dan Steely, his case on his lap,
Sat on the omnibus taking a nap.
The shiny black tyres, they whined underneath.
But Arthur was shattered and so were his teeth.
He trudged up his street in the fast fading light;
His wife, who'd stopped laughing, said, "You're late tonight.
I poured you a Guinness to drown all your sorrow —
We'll just have to hope you're discovered tomorrow!"

Ayers Rock

How with only a meat pie and a pair of tennis shoes, the fearless poet scaled the vertical face of Ayers Rock and learned to exaggerate in the process.

Daybreak over Ayers Rock —
The Centre's breath was baited.
Snakes slid down their tunnels
And a huntsman spider waited.
Little grieving redbacks wandered,
Never could they rest:
Searching, ever searching
For the seat they loved the best.

But an enigmatic figure
Stood beside the Uluru,
With one lip curled in scorn
The way the real explorers do.
The day was growing hotter
But she calmly scanned the skies,
Covered up with 'Aeroguard'
And half-a-million flies.

She wore her expedition clothes —
She'd planned this day for months:
The shorts that Burke and Wills
Could both have travelled in at once,
The tennis shoes Bjorn Borg
Had signed along the side —
Behold! Pam Ayres the Mountaineer!
Oh! Speak her name with pride!

I set out from the Uluru
All in my digger's hat,
And forty others set out
But we won't go into that.
I scaled the mighty mountainside
And folks we chanced to meet
Cried out, "Here comes Pam Ayres!
She must have suckers on her feet!"

I was frank and I was fearless,
I threw away my coat
And, lunging for the summit,
I was like a mountain goat.
A party from Whyalla
Was clinging to the chain
And hollered down the line,
"She's overtaking us...again!"

But the vista from the summit
Was a marvel to behold.
I signed the special book
Although my hands were stiff with cold.
The mighty Olgas slumbered on
So beautiful and round
As though a giant horse had paused
To fertilise the ground.

Yet as I stood surveying
This extraordinary place,
I thought I felt a drop of rain
Roughly smite me face.
The skies began to open,
My heart began to sink
And in five minutes time
Ayers Rock was like a skating rink.

The Bjorn Borgs were sodden
They'd cost me oh so dear!
He might have helped on the Centre Court
But he couldn't help me here.
I couldn't get a purchase!
I couldn't get a grip!
And everywhere I placed me feet
Me feet began to slip!

There was nothing to hold on to!
I quickly gave up hope.
In my imagination
I fell screaming down the slope.
I heard me mother weeping
As she clutched my digger's hat,
I heard the poets of the world
Say, "Thank the Lord for that!"

I said to my companion,
"Will you see I get a plaque?
Not the dental kind
The one for not arriving back.
Fix it high above the road,
Write 'Poet of Renown:
Pam Ayres the Ayers Rock heroine
Who slipped up coming down'."

But in the end I didn't falter
Though my shoes had lost their soles,
Though the shorts that Burke and Wills
Could both have worn were shot with holes,
But if I hadn't made it
And downwards had been hurled
At least I would have had
The biggest headstone in the world!

Clothes Brush Tango

There's nothing like a dog
For bringing dog hair in the house.
Dog hair round your dear old Dad
And dog hair round your spouse,
Dog hair down your trouser leg
Despite me cries of warning;
I might as well get drunk tonight
'Cause it's hair of the dog in the morning!

Heaps of Stuff

How I wish that I was tidy
How I wish that I was neat
How I wish I was methodical
Like others down our street.
I tried to stem the rising tide
I tried to hold it back
But I have been the victim
Of a heap of stuff attack.

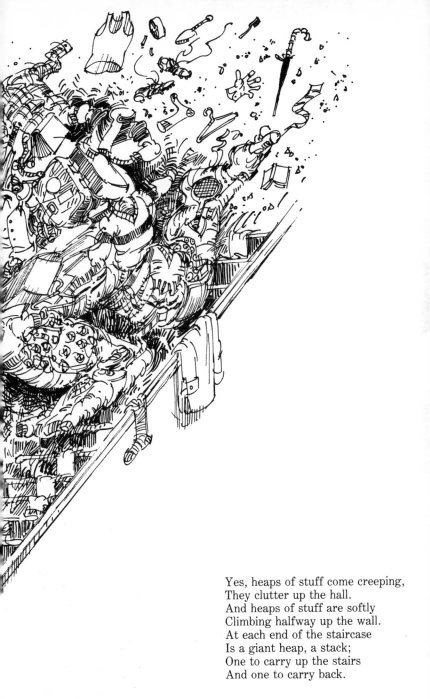

Yes, heaps of stuff come creeping,
They clutter up the hall.
And heaps of stuff are softly
Climbing halfway up the wall.
At each end of the staircase
Is a giant heap, a stack;
One to carry up the stairs
And one to carry back.

In a heap of stuff invasion
They settle everywhere —
They grovel on the lino
They tower on the chair.
You're searching for a jacket,
"Is it in here?" you shout,
And, opening the cupboard door,
A heap of stuff falls out.

But heaps are many-faceted
And heaps are multi-faced
And what a heap is made of
Will depend on where it's placed.
Now if it's in the passage
It is mostly boots and shoes
And if it's on the sofa
It is magazines and news.

If it's in the shed
It's broken propagating frames
And if it's in the bathroom
Well, it's best to say no names,
And if it's in the bedroom —
Your own and not the guest's —
The heap of stuff is mostly made
Of sock and shirts and vests.

For a heap is indestructible,
It's something you can't fight.
If you split it up by day
It joins back up at night.
So cunningly positioned
As from room to room you trek,
Increasing all the chances
That you trip and break your neck.

But step into my parlour
Now I've forced the door ajar;
I'll excavate an easy chair —
Just cling there where you are.
And together we'll survey it
Till our eyes they feast enough
On the tidiest home in England
Underneath the heaps of stuff.

Play Us A Tune On Your Whistle, Father, I've Lost Another Stone

Some days I'm so clever at slimming
Some days I eat nothing at all
And my stomach feels ever so hollow
And me waistline feels ever so small.
Perhaps it does get a bit boring —
Calorie counting is dull
But some days my face is so lovely and thin
That it's like staring back at a skull.

How I love both my hip bones protruding
How I worship my knobbly knees
And laying out in my bikini
Me ribs play a tune in the breeze.
Mind, I have to take care with me elbows
For they've gone in the shape of a peak,
And the last time I nudged me poor husband
He never stood up for a week.

How I love the great flaps round me midriff
Where fat once it blubbered and sang.
Now these great folds of skin have nothing within
And about me they tastefully hang.
For that's one disadvantage of slimming —
It can make the skin somewhat slack
And as I have no wish to frighten the dog
I tend to go round in my 'mac.

Now some women fantasise nightly
Of erotic adventures and steam
But without sounding drab, all I want to grab
Is a bucket or two of ice-cream.
But you got to keep up with the fashion
You got to look lissom and lean.
You'll swoon at me lovely bone structure
When I've shifted the stuff in between.

Oh, but look at me glorious bottom.
A stone from around it I've cropped
And so once again its a lovely size 10
(If only it hadn't have dropped).
Yes! slimming's enhanced me composure
But it hasn't enhanced me jawline —
You think you've seen wattles on turkeys?
Well, brother, you want to see mine!

Goodbye to my little old corset
There's nothing for you to restrain
Thanks to my cellulose biscuits
In onion and chocolate and plain.
Here's to the hunger suppressors
As I bid you farewell and adieu;
Here's hoping you'll soon see less of me
And I'll see nothing of you.

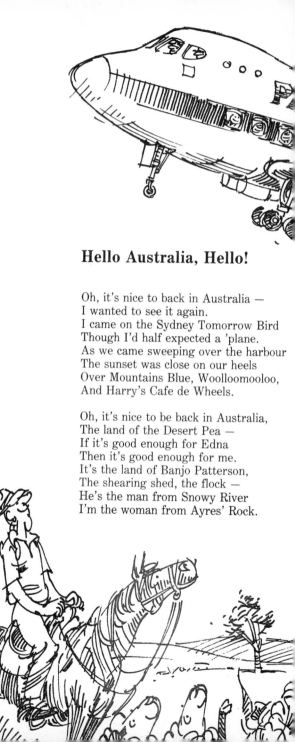

Hello Australia, Hello!

Oh, it's nice to back in Australia —
I wanted to see it again.
I came on the Sydney Tomorrow Bird
Though I'd half expected a 'plane.
As we came sweeping over the harbour
The sunset was close on our heels
Over Mountains Blue, Woolloomooloo,
And Harry's Cafe de Wheels.

Oh, it's nice to be back in Australia,
The land of the Desert Pea —
If it's good enough for Edna
Then it's good enough for me.
It's the land of Banjo Patterson,
The shearing shed, the flock —
He's the man from Snowy River
I'm the woman from Ayres' Rock.

Oh, pass me that Pavlova
All drenched in kiwi fruit,
And drive me out in the mulga
With a roo bar on the ute,
And underneath a stringybark
I'll see what passes through —
A currawong might fly along
And the odd thorn-bird or two.

Oh, the Lamingtons bloom in Sydney
And food no-one can resist
Which might be why each man goes by
With a meat pie in his fist.
I'm glad to be back in Australia
And it'll be beaut I know
If I see you about, I'll pick up the shout,
Hello Australia, Hello!

Eat, Drink and Be Sick

Well, Happy Christmas, Father,
Have I got a treat for you!
A pair of socks in bottle green
And one in navy blue.
I wrapped them round your after-shave
And put them by the tree
And wrote me name in biro
So you'd know they came from me.

Well yes, I'll have a mince pie please
And then I'll have a date
And then I'll crack a nut or two
And fling them in the grate,
And then I'll have a fig
And then perhaps a glass of wine
And then another two or three
To make me forehead shine.

One cold turkey sandwich
But a *small* one, understand.
Look, the meat's all falling out —
You got a rubber band?
Stoke the fire up, Father,
Ram the poker down the back,
Those potatoes in the ashes
Well, they've never looked so black!

Well yes, I'll have a liqueur chocolate
With the crunchy sugar coat
That rattles round your teeth
And turns to gravel in your throat.
How nice the room looks, Mother,
With the tinsel round the walls,
I'll have an Advocaat then please,
Yes, that one there, the Bols.

Just one slice of Christmas cake
Then I shall have to run.
A tangerine then, if you *must* —
Just hold this Chelsea bun.
One glass of cherry brandy
No more crystal fruits for me!
Happy Christmas all!
I'm going home to have me tea!

Plughole Serenade

Would you care to come sailing with me love,
For the wind couldn't puff out a candle.
We'll drag the tin bath up the old garden path
And you have the end with the handle.

How God Made the Duck-Billed Platypus

The duck-billed platypus, small aquatic friend
Made from the pieces God had over at the end.
According to His reckoning (He'd not been wrong before)
He hadn't made enough: He needed one mammal more.

He studied all the corners in his cupboard large and bare
A little foot here, and a little nose there,
A scrap of fur, a feather, nothing anyone would miss
And God said, "Oh Good God...Yes?...What can I make out of this?"

There was a funny flat tail and a great enormous beak
Which had lain in the cupboard for a year and a week,
There were four webbed feet in the manner of a duck
And hanging on a peg a furry overcoat for luck!

So the turn of the platypus came to be fitted
God sat him down and he honestly admitted
That the finished platypus might appear a little odd,
"But look on the bright side of it," said God.

You can swim in the river, you can paddle in the creek,
You can tackle *anybody* with a great big beak,
There's a tail for a rudder or alternatively legs
And by way of consolation you've got babies *and* eggs.

So God took all the pieces into Workshop One
And there he told the men the sort of thing he wanted done.
The Carpenter and Plumber stroked the platypus's neck
And said, "Don't you upset him, he can't run but he can peck!"

So the platypus was made, and his beak was firmly rooted,
And God found him a home where he would not be persecuted.
They packed him up and sent him with his tail neatly furled
In a brown paper parcel marked "Australia, The World".

Gold! Gold! Under the Church

In Barkerville long, long ago
Men struck gold and in the glow
Of their new wealth they felt so good
They built a church and there it stood.

All around the church they mined,
Round the front and up behind,
In summer heat and winter cold
They stripped and raped the land of gold.

The seam ran out it came to pass,
The goldfield sprouted tufts of grass.
But as prospectors set to leave
A voice rang "Stop, I believe...

That even though we mined the town
Inside out and upside down
There's one spot yet we did not search
There's gold under that thar church!''

The vicar would not hear of it,
"Get out!" he roared, "You hypocrite!
Perhaps I *shall* drop down to hell
But I shan't go down in the church as well!''

The miners begged and they implored,
They lifted up the odd floorboard
And swore their brand of ventilation
Would surely save the congregation.

Men ran fore and men ran aft
Could they...would they...sink a shaft?
And, when standing in the pew,
What was the chance of falling through?

Oh! Ecclesiastics not inclined
To have your chancel undermined
Learn from this fight that's gone before
And build *your* church on iron-ore.

Hello Long Distance, Is That You?

Hello? Hello? Hello? Hello?
Oh, hello Mum! It's *me!*
Hello! How are you keeping?
Yes, I can. Can you hear me?
How is everybody? Alright?
Yes and we are too.
It's twenty-five past seven here —
What time is it with you?

Ay? Dad would like a word?
Oh, he's just coming on, I see.
Hello! How are you Dad?
Oh yes I *can*. Can you hear me?
How is everybody? Alright?
Yes, and we are too.
Twenty-five past seven, Dad,
What time is it with you?

Well, Dad, how's the weather?
How's the weather, nice I s'pose?
I said how-is-the-weather?
How's the WEATHER? (Stone the crows!)
Dad? Just call to Mum,
I think she's on the bedroom 'phone.
I can't hear you *both*
Tell her to leave that one alone.

Ay? Who asked me that?
Was that you Dad? Oh, it was Mum.
Twenty-five past seven here —
Rain? Yes, we're getting some.
Well, it rained up to the Wednesday
'Cause I had the ear-ache
And then it brightened up...
No! It was Thursday (my mistake).

We had this thunderstorm:
It scared us all out of our wits.
Oh, it upset Mrs. White —
That Mrs. White who has the fits... no FITS!
Hello? I thought I'd lost you —
No, I'd got the dialling tone.
Try not to shout so loud Dad,
Dad? Why don't you use the phone?

All right then, better go then
Or we shan't afford the bill.
Just *gone* half-past-seven, Dad,
So long then... Yes we will,
All the best, mind how you go
And Dad? Stay off the booze!
Enjoy the rain, I'll ring again
Next time I've got some news.

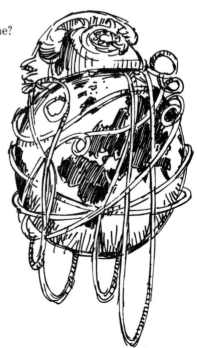

Miss Grundy and the Grand Hotel

Miss Grundy ran the Grand Hotel.
She called it grand but you couldn't tell
For it was very dark and drear
And dust stood thick on the chandelier.
The carpets once so plush and fine
Were full of holes and dust and wine
And the wallpaper embossed and plain
Had rolled itself back up again.

No music flowed in the marble halls,
No Gala Nights, Midsummer Balls,
Since the night when the Town and Country Planner
Poured his beer down the old pianner.
No smile ever cracked the receptionist's face
But the smell of her nail polish oozed through the place
And, mixed with the fragrance of frying, it rose
To deal the hotel guests a punch on the nose.

Soon however the plot of land
Next door to the crumbling Grand
Came up for sale and folks heard tell
That there were new plans for a new hotel.
Miss Grundy didn't care a jot
But sniffed, "My regulars I've got.
They'd never dream of leaving here
They pay through the nose for the atmosphere!"

But they watched with wary eyes
As the new hotel blocked out the skies.
The receptionist, afire with dread,
Changed her nails from pink to red.
Not only had it H & C,
All mod cons and colour TV,
But taking shape along the corner
Was a brand new swimming pool...and sauna!

Miss Grundy, deciding to put up a fight,
Took a broom to the chandelier one night
And so that people could get up late
Didn't *stop* breakfast till quarter to eight.
To enable the music and dancing to start
She stood up one night and sang "Heart of my Heart",
She hung up pictures of highland cattle
Miss Grundy alas fought a losing battle.

For the guests at the Grand Hotel saw the light
And all tunnelled out under cover of night
Under the room where Miss Grundy snored,
Where the mousetraps guarded the skirting board,
Into the warmth of the one next door,
The swimming pool and the carpet floor,
While outside stirring in the chilly breeze
Miss Grundy's sign read "Vacancies".

Lost in Transit

I left my heart in Australia
I left my knees in Japan
I left my liver
Up the Yangtze River
And I'm only half a man.

Please Will You Take Your Children Home Before I Do Them In

Please will you take your children home
Before I do them in?
I kissed your little son
As he came posturing within.
I took his little jacket
And removed his little hat
But now the visit's over
So push off you little brat.

And don't think for a moment
That I didn't understand
How the hatchet he was waving
In his grotty little hand
Broke my china teapot
That I've always held so dear —
But would you mind removing him
Before I smack his ear?

Of course I wasn't angry
As I shovelled up the dregs,
I'm only glad the teabags
Didn't scald his little legs.
I'm glad he liked my chocolate cake
I couldn't help but laugh
As he rubbed it in the carpet...
Would he like the other half?

He guzzled all the orange
And he guzzled all the Coke —
The only thing that kept me sane
Was hoping he might choke.
And then he had a mishap,
Well, I couldn't bear to look,
Do something for your Auntie little sunshine...
Sling your hook.

He's been playing in the garden
And he's throttled all the flowers,
Give the lad a marlinspike
He'll sit out there for hours.
I've gathered my insecticides
And marked them with their name
And put them up where children
Couldn't reach them. That's a shame.

Still he must have liked my dog
Because he choked her half to death,
She'll go out for another game
Once she's caught her breath.
He rode her round the garden
And he lashed her with his rope
She's never bitten anyone
But still, we live in hope.

He's kicked the TV now!
I like to see it getting booted
Kick it one more time son
You might get electrocuted!
Yes, turn up the volume,
Twist the knobs, me little treasure
And when the programme's over
There's the door. It's been a pleasure.

The Beach Lovers

Come and walk beside me
For the sun is sinking low
And together to the edges
Of the ocean we shall go,
And all our rosy future
In perspective we shall put
Stepping lightly on the rubbish
As it moulders underfoot.
Where all the plastic bottles
Blow across the golden sand
And old refrigerators
Know the tide's caressing hand,
We will breathe the sweet aroma,
I will take your hand for ever,
Across life's broken glass,
And I shall jettison you never.

I'm The Dog Who Didn't Win a Prize

I'm the dog who didn't win a prize.
I didn't have the Most Appealing Eyes.
All day in this heat, I've been standing on me feet
With dogs of every other shape and size.

I've been harshly disinfected, I've been scrubbed,
I've been festooned in a towel and I've been rubbed;
I've been mercilessly brushed, robbed of all me fleas and dust
And now the judging's over: I've been snubbed!

Was it for obedience I was hailed?
As "Best Dog in the Show" was I regaled?
O not on your Doggo life, pass me down the carving knife,
I had one thing said about me — it was "FAILED".

I never for a moment thought I'd fail.
I thought at least I'd win "Waggiest Tail".
But no certificate, rosette or commendation did I get —
Nothing on a kennel door to nail.

I am going in my kennel on my own.
Thank you, no. I do not want a bone.
Do not think you can console me with left-overs in my bowl me
pride is mortified: I want to be alone.

I've heard it from the worldly and the wise:
"Each dog has his day" they all advise,
But I see to my grief and sorrow, my day must have been tomorrow!
Oh I'm the dog who didn't win a prize!

Up The Spout

Man is gloriously clever
Making intricate machines
And complicated gadgetry
And bigger runner beans
And journeys into space
With mighty rockets in the tail —
But when the last one's towed away
He couldn't make

        a whale.

Mary Boggis Clark

Mary Boggis Clark from the top of Hatcher's End
Married Henry Crocker for a mentor and a friend.

She clung to Henry Crocker's arm when going for a stroll
For Mary Boggis Clark, she was a nervous little soul.

When they were recumbent in their feather marriage bed
Henry Crocker reached across to fondle Mary's head

Imagine his surprise when Mary Clark began to scream
Explaining she had just been getting strangled in a dream.

And Mary Boggis Clark, she did not improve at all
From seeing faces in the dark and shadows on the wall.

Mary graduated to hallucinations better
And conjured up all kinds of things that came at night to get her;

And Henry's fond advances, they were rather brushed aside
And Henry's private yearnings — well, they went unsatisfied.

Sometimes he tried to give her a preliminary peck
But the old familiar prickling on the back of Mary's neck

Would cause her to forget him crying, "Henry! Henry! Hark!
I do believe there's someone creeping up here in the dark!"

Now very soon it all began to get on Henry's wick
He tired of Mary shouting, "Henry! Henry! Wake up quick!"

He tired of groping half asleep at midnight round the room
In search of Mary's spectres as they rose up from the gloom.

He couldn't *hear* the bumping or the rattlers and bangers
That Mary said was spirits, phantoms, ghouls and dopplegangers.

Mary was so nervous it was difficult to leave her
Specially as beside the bed she kept the mutton cleaver.

With such frequent visitations Henry couldn't keep apace
And he watched in mute amazement as she cleavered round the place.

Mary went to pictures just for something fresh to do
She found the film was *Werewolf in the Graveyard Meets Kung Fu.*

She didn't want to see it and her courage drained away
So she sat for ninety minutes trying to look the other way.

She came out of the pictures and her face was pale with fright
Darting nervous over-shoulder glances left and right.

She scuttled down the cobbles by the green and oily cut
Thinking she was safely home to Henry Crocker. But...

She saw a figure moving on the water's other side —
A young man crept in view, his eyes were panicky and wide,

He stared at Mary Boggis Clark and jumped and cried, "Oh no!"
And cringed beneath the street lamp in its pale and ghostly glow.

Mary strained her eyes to see, for all the lane was dim
She knew that she was scared but she was not as scared as him,

She stepped across the bridge and laid her hand upon his arm
For he was white and frightened...but he had a certain charm.

"Good lady" cried the man, "That you should see me in this state,
I never should have ventured from my home this far, this late;

For what handicaps my life and makes me eminently kickable
Is my fear of the supernatural and inexplicable."

He said, "I cannot walk the street or anywhere at all
Without this constant fear that round the back of every wall,

Listening for footsteps, crouched in menacing positions,
Are poltergeists and spooks and paranormal apparitions

And once outside my door, I found the sign, the Living Proof
For printed in the garden, there it was, the Cloven Hoof.

Although I will admit this theory was placed in doubt
For it coincided with the day me bullocks all got out,

Fear is what I live with of the most illogic kind,
Fear of being suddenly garotted from behind,

Fear of hooded phantoms that across the water float
To nod and wink and clench their bony fingers round me throat."

Mary gazed about her and her face was white with joy
And she told him, "You are not alone, I'm just the same...my boy."

And they began to tremble now the wondrous truth was known
They trembled both at once and then he trembled on his own.

"Oh," sighed Mary Boggis Clark with unrestrained relief,
"I am so greatly comforted, for it was my belief

That all through life alone I must these apparitions meet.
Come home with me and we'll throw Henry's things out in the street.

I know he is my husband but still the outlook's grim
For statistics prove if someone's going to murder me...it's *him!*"

"But I'm scared of my own shadow!" wailed the man and hung his head
But Mary Boggis Clark said, "So am I" and they were wed!

And went on honeymoon where in the warm and sunny weather,
Hand in hand for life, they will be seeing things together.